Eclipse Of The Heart

Shamarah Richmond

BookLeaf Publishing

India | USA | UK

Eclipse Of The Heart © 2024 Shamarah
Richmond

All rights reserved.

No part of this publication may be
reproduced, stored in a retrieval system, or
transmitted, in any form or by any means,
electronic, mechanical, photocopying,
recording or otherwise, without the prior
written permission of the presenters.

Shamarah Richmond asserts the moral right
to be identified as author of this work.

Presentation by *BookLeaf Publishing*

Web: www.bookleafpub.com

E-mail: info@bookleafpub.com

ISBN: 9789363311886

First edition 2024

*Dedicated to flowers and bees and hot
chocolate and people who are full of whimsy.*

Wish Exploration

Phases of life,
eclipsing one another.
There must be moments of darkness
before the sun can uncover.

Make eye contact with the moon,
let your eyes explore,
to reveal everything
you truly wish for.

Bayou Treading

You will get stuck in murky water .
it is inevitable,
don't fight it.
Live in it, for just a moment.
Let the moss brush your cheeks,
the humid air kiss your eyelids,
only then will the vines let go
and you can continue down the bayou.

A Plea

I can't hear myself think
in the quietest moments I'm graced with.
A privilege for the rich,
to discuss their stolen ideas.
Everyday we're tortured
for reasons we could never touch,
honestly it's tiring but silly,
like god can hold a grudge.

Just need to keep going,
so i can reach those peaceful moments.
Surely they exist, right?
Please just let me hold them.

Set Me Free

Set me free,
though I know my wings aren't full.
Let me explore the horrible world that lies
ahead.
Set me free,
let me choose to give up,
let me out of orbit,
don't hold on to me.
Let me explore the possible galaxies waiting to
love me.

Till Death Do I Part

On New Years Eve,
On the first snow,
Under the mistletoe,
Under the cherry blossoms,
On the beach under the strawberry moon,
I'll be there for myself every time.

The Winning Model

If no sleep is the cost of the medal,
I'll happily lose the hours
because i cant afford the time.
Even in burnout,
I'll have to keep going
because nothing I own is mine.
I'll keep running
towards something unknown
because there was never a finish line.

Let Me In

Outside of the storm,
when the window shakes,
I feel no fear.
Only comfort,
I know nature is near
yet i cant be touched
in my manmade obstruction.
It's beautiful isn't it?
to be protected?
But is it protection or is it encasing?
when in the heart of the storm,
it's terrifying.
Yet it's the time you feel most alive.
When you touch sand or mud or rock
You can feel the earth calling you back.
Almost makes you miss the place you're living
on,
even though it never went anywhere.
It stays, Yet, we're the ones who push it away.

My Daily Sugar

In the midst of the crowds I see them
they'll never see me,
most likely.
Yet they know me?
They can sense my fears and hesitations,
pushing me to reach through them like water
to reach my most horrifying desires.
Through our conversations,
I've learned to run without destination.
I've slowly been taught it's the only way to move
when i feel stuck in the crowd,
or in the system I've been pushed into
since the existence of the star I'm born out of.

The Monster Is Still me

Frankenstein's monster and I would've been
great friends.
Both monsters looking inside,
wishing to be understood,
learning the insides and outs of humans
without being able to experience the love of
humanity for ourselves.
Forever wishing for love
with the monsters that created us leaving us to
the hands of loneliness
as punishments for crimes
we were subjected to commit.

Celestial Interlude

Saturn is slowly losing it's rings. In around 150 million years most of it's rings will be gone. It makes me think about the fact that celestial bodies also experience loss. Planets lose moons, rings fall out of orbit, pluto was deemed not good enough to be a planet. Humans arent the only ones experiencing loss everyday. If anything, we experience loss at a much smaller scale. It's never easy to let go, but stars are ripped away from blackholes to never return. If Saturn can let go of its rings, I can let go of moments in my short, short life.

Hello World

hello world
this is me
in all my parts
if you see me
on the street
you wont
see it all
not even close
hello world
do i even exist
outside of this screen
why cant i be the real me
i'll scroll until i die
looking for an answer
hello world

An Interview

Does the tired ever end?
Do i ever chase what will satisfy me?
Or continue to chase what will momentarily
fulfill my hunger?
Will I ever stop looking for what will make me
happy
and start looking for what will change the way I
see the world?
Do I know myself enough to not hate what I
see?
- With Reverence

The First Step is to Take The First Step

The greatest unknown of our existence,
the First Step.

"Take the First Step."
"Don't be afraid of falling."
"Don't be afraid to fail."
"Take the First Step."
"Test the waters."
Have you ever been on that edge?
Where you don't even know what the First Step
is? Or if you've already taken it?
Everyone says "take the First Step" but no one
talks about how mundane the first step feels. It
feels like I haven't taken any steps fifteen steps
in. Like I've been running down a dark road that
won't actually take me anywhere.
Maybe I was so focused on the First Step that i
forgot the real first step was to grab a map and a
flashlight

Bumble Bee

The candied honey coating my tongue,
the hazy memories that follow me as I run,
knowing that if i wanted
I could ruin this for fun.
Press your thumbs below my ribs to feel where
my fears lie
theres so many there, please don't be disgusted if
I start to cry.

Forgetfullness

Oh God,
isn't it so easy to forget?
That we are one with the sun
and the dirt,
the soil,
the grass,
the rivers,
the lakes,
the waterfalls,
the trees,
and the stars!!!
We've coexisted for so long that they must know
us by know such as we know them,
but it's horrifyingly easy to forget
when the trees are overshadowed by buildings
and everyday access to yards with plush grass is
reserved for the wealthy.
When we can look up in the night sky
and not see the families of stars,
it suddenly becomes terribly easy to forget.

Desire Will Surely Kill

me
slowly
slowly
slowly
for every ache in my chest is driven by desire
but so is the motivation to live another second.

Work-Life-Work-Work Balance

Work to live and live to work,
the machine wants me to be tired.
Using whatever content i can consume the
fastest
to numb the pain of being caught in this decades
long trap.
Work so much that I forget
who I even am,
what I even like,
or whats ever brought me genuine joy.
It's the same giants feeding me problems who try
to feed me solutions designed to keep me alive
enough to be working, but not alive enough to
realize I'm stuck, and not nearly alive enough to
have the energy to do anything about it.

That's All?

Is this the end?
Is this it?
Work to die and play to live
and live till you can't feel it.
Can't feel the crushing weight
of simple existence.
when what should be easy
has a heavy resonance.

Roapocalypse

Dance around in your room,
live a little more.
Don't stop
even if meteors come crashing through.
They can't stop the light
you exude into this universe

The Stars Are Listening

The message is everywhere,
loud and clear.
Don't you dare ignore it,
instead hold it dear.

The end isn't the purpose.
The journey is why you're here.
Nothing can be planned.
Life is played by ear.

It will be scary in the unknown
but don't hold on to fear .
When you're most in need
the universe will hear.

Accelerate Harder

In the end what's most important is remembering just how much you love to love. how much you look forward to taking care of yourself and others. How much room and time there is to connect with others. Your life isn't over yet. Darling, it's barely even started. It's much, much too early to give up on something this good. Keep making mistakes, but try to go a little bit lighter on yourself. Don't hurt yourself so much for wanting to experience this world in it's fullest and all it has to offer. Don't ignore that, it's your desire to live and explore banging on your front door. So continue to chase miscellaneous dreams that seem out of reach. If not for you, then for me.

www.ingramcontent.com/pod-product-compliance
Lightning Source LLC
LaVergne TN
LVHW050306200726
843509LV00015B/3180